BICYCLES

Authors: George and Shirley Coulter

Rourke Publications, Inc.
Vero Beach, Florida 32964

About the Authors
Award-winning teachers in the state of Wisconsin, George and Shirley Coulter have now retired,
but remain active in the field of science education, designing and presenting teacher workshops.
Both are published authors of books and articles in national, professional journals in the field
of science education.

A book by Market Square Communications Incorporated
Pamela J.P. Schroeder, Editor
Sandra J. Shekels, Illustrator

Photo Credits
Pages 7 and 23 courtesy of TREK USA; page 21 © photo by Gork.

Acknowledgements
Thanks to Campus Cycle, Stevens Point, WI, for providing cycling
equipment for use in photos.

Library of Congress Cataloging-in-Publication Data
Coulter, George, 1934-
    Bicycles / authors, George and Shirley Coulter.
       p. cm. — (You make it work)
    Includes index.
    Summary: Explains the scientific principles that make bicycles
move and how various parts of a bicycle work and examines different kinds
of bicycles.
    ISBN 0-86625-587-7
    1. Bicycles—Juvenile literature. [1. Bicycles.] I. Coulter, Shirley, 1936-.
II. Title. III. Series: Coulter, George, 1934- . You make it work.
TL540.C68 1996
629.227'2—dc20   96-7516
                                    CIP
                                     AC

Printed in the USA

Illustrations are simplified examples meant to show general concepts
rather than specific technical detail.

TABLE OF CONTENTS

CHAPTER ONE

GEAR UP WITH BICYCLES

Somewhere outside, in the garage or on the driveway, is there a bicycle with your name on it? What kind of bike is it? What would your dream bike be like?

The great thing about bikes is that they can really make your neighborhood bigger. You can go a lot farther in a lot shorter time than you can on foot.

Bicycles can give you more freedom to move around, but they also come with more responsibility. You have to know and follow the rules of the road. Plus, you need to know how to take care of your bicycle.

Without you, bicycles are just piles of metal, plastic and **gears** (GEERZ). With your feet at the pedals, a bike can become a racing machine, a mountain climber, or just a way to get from here to there. It's your choice.

Bicycles have come a long way since the first one was invented way back in the 1790s. That first bike had no pedals or handlebars. You aimed it in the right direction and pushed with your feet. If you were lucky, the bike actually went where you wanted it to go.

Bicycle Boom

Today, in the United States alone, there are between 80 and 90 million bicycles—that's one for every three people!

In Europe, bicycle road racing is the most popular summer sport. However, China is the biking capital of the world. More people in China own bikes than in any other country. In fact, there are more bikes than cars on the road in China!

Bicycles need you even more than you need them. If you take good care of them, they'll take good care of you while you're on, or off, the road.

Later, people added handles for steering and pedals for leg power. In the 1970s, bicycles got a popularity push when the **derailleur** (di RAY lur) gear system, or multiple gears, was added. People started to realize how bikes could help them get into shape. Even grandmothers and grandfathers got into it!

In this book, you'll find out about the science that makes bicycles move. You'll get a first-hand look at how each part of a bike works, and how they work together. You'll explore different kinds of bikes, and how they're used. Also, you'll discover how bicycles can be so alike and so different at the same time.

Let's blaze a new trail with bicycles!

5

CHAPTER TWO

BEFORE YOU RIDE

What's the first thing you do before you take a bike ride? Safety equipment aside, the first thing most people do is grab the handlebars, put up the kickstand, and take a seat.

The Seat

What's the first thing you think about when you hear the word *bike?* It may not be the seat, but seats are very important. How long could you stay on your bike without one?

The longer you ride, the more important your seat, or saddle, gets. Bicycle seats come in all shapes and sizes—small and thin racing seats, long banana seats, saddle-shaped seats, and so on. Pick one that works best for you.

Your bike seat and feet will tell if your bike is the right size for you. If you can sit on the seat and touch the ground with your feet, you have a perfect fit. If your feet don't touch, or if your legs bend, you'll need to adjust your seat up or down.

A Bike-King Champion

Greg LeMond might be one of the best road racers ever! He was the first American to win the famous Tour de France. The Tour de France is over 2,300 miles long. It takes about three weeks for the racers to finish. Since his first victory, Greg won the race two more times!

Racing bikes have special parts to help them go faster. However, they work the same way that street bikes or mountain bikes do.

Seat

The frame of a bike is like your skeleton.
It supports all the parts of your bicycle.

Seat Stay

Back Cantilever
Brakes

Seat
Tube

Axle

Gearwheels

Back Wheel

Derailleur

Chainwheel

Back Tire

PARTS OF YOUR BIKE

Handlebars

Handlebar Stem

Top Tube

Down Tube

Front Cantilever
Brakes

Front Wheel
Fork

Front Wheel

Pedal

Front Tire

Your handlebars are your control center. From there, you can steer, stop and switch gears.

The Handlebars

The most obvious use for handlebars is steering. They are attached tightly to the handlebar stem with a bolt. When you turn the handlebars, the front wheel turns in the same direction. However, handlebars are important in helping you balance, too. It's much easier, and safer, to ride your bike using two hands.

You'll also find **gear** levers and brake levers on the handlebars. They are like the control center for your bike. You can slow down, switch gears or stop. You can also add a light or a horn to your handlebars. Horns and lights let other people know where you are.

Handlebars with grips are the best kind. Handle grips help you hang on without slipping. They can also keep you from getting cut on the metal edge of the handlebars if you fall.

Handlebars can add a little style to your bike, too. You can choose dropped, curved handlebars, like on a racing bike. There are the flat, short handlebars on a dirt or mountain bike, or high handlebars.

The Frame

Your seat and handlebars are both attached to the bike's frame. The frame of a bicycle is like a skeleton. The muscles that help you move are attached to the bones in your skeleton. The parts of a bike that help it move are attached to its frame.

Most frames are made of metal **alloy** (A loy) tubing. Metal makes the frame strong. However, a solid metal frame would be very heavy, and need a lot of pedal power to make it move. Metal tubing is lightweight, and strong, too. Carbon fiber is another strong, light material people use to make frames.

Over the front wheel are the *front wheel fork* and the *handlebar stem*. They turn and let you steer with the help of **bearings** (BAYR ingz). The *down tube* goes back from the handlebars. Some bikes also have a *top tube,* or *cross bar.*

The down tube reaches down to the **chainwheel** (CHAYN weel). That's where your pedals are attached. Inside the chainwheel is the spindle, or **axle** (AK sul). It turns because of bearings, too.

The *seat tube* comes up from the chainwheel. Of course, you put your seat in the top of the seat tube. Finally, leading back from the seat tube is the *seat stay.* The seat stay connects to the gear in the back wheel.

Everything you need to drive a bike connects to the frame—the wheels, the brakes, fenders—everything.

Biking For A Living

In large cities, some people make their living by delivering messages— by bicycle. They bike from business to business along busy city streets to deliver important messages quickly.

Adding To Your Bike

There are lots of things you can buy to make your bike yours and nobody else's. You can add things to make your bike look just the way you want it—and make it more safe, too.

Lights and reflectors. If you want to ride your bike at night, it's a good idea to have a headlight and lots of reflectors. You can get lights that run from battery power.

Some lights work from the energy you make yourself when you ride your bike. A small **generator** (JEH nu ray tur) attaches to your wheel. It turns the motion energy from your turning wheel into electrical energy to run your light.

It's a good idea to put reflectors on your pedals and in the spokes of your wheels. Add some reflector tape on your clothing, and you'll be easy to spot.

Bike reflectors are made of clear plastic—usually red or white. The outside of a reflector is smooth. However, the inside is covered by many small prisms. Light comes in the reflector, reflects from a prism and bounces into another prism. Then the light reflects off the second prism and bounces out of the reflector. The light bouncing off of many prisms inside makes the reflector seem to glow.

Speedometers and odometers. When you're riding, do you ever wonder how fast you're going? Speedometers can tell you just that.

Most bike speedometers are computerized today. Inside is a **microprocessor** (mii kroh PRAHS es ur), or mini computer. The first thing you need to do is tell the microprocessor the wheel size of your bike, and if you want to see your speed in miles-per-hour or kilometers-per-hour.

Early Rules Of The Road

In 1819, New York City passed a law making it illegal to use velocipedes —an early form of bicycle—in public places and on the sidewalks of the city.

A cable runs from the microprocessor on your handlebars to a sensor on your front wheel fork. There is also a magnet on the spokes of your front wheel. As your front wheel turns, the magnet goes past the sensor. Then the sensor sends a signal to the microprocessor. The microprocessor uses these signals to measure speed.

Some speedometers can also tell you the time and how long you've been riding. Most speedometers come with an odometer. Odometers tell you how far you've gone.

Locks and security chains. Thousands of bicycles are stolen in the United States every year. A good lock and **security** (si KYUR uh tee) chain can help you protect your bike. However, you need to be sure to lock your bike up tight. The chain should go through both your wheels and around the frame, and around the bike rack.

To lock up your bike tight, make sure to run your security chain around the frame and through both tires, too.

CHAPTER THREE

ON THE MOVE

Up goes the kickstand. Push off with your feet—and you're on your way!

What actually happens when you push the pedals? How does your bike turn your leg power into speed and motion? The pedals you push with your feet are really part of a **crank** (KRANK) in the **chainwheel.** So when you push the pedals, they crank the chainwheel around.

The chainwheel is a **sprocket** (SPRAH kut) with teeth to hold a chain. The chain goes around both the chainwheel and the **freewheel** (FREE weel) in the back wheel. As the chainwheel turns, so does the chain. The chain turns the freewheel, and the freewheel turns the back wheel.

You might have noticed how the freewheel, or **gears,** in the back wheel are much smaller than the chainwheel. Because the freewheel is smaller, it goes around faster than the chainwheel. That means that as you pedal, your back wheel goes around faster than you're pedaling.

What job does each part of your bicycle play in moving you down the road?

The Pedals

The pedals are what turn your leg power into speed. They're the handles of the crank that make the chainwheel go around. As you already know, it's the chainwheel that gets everything started.

There are two kinds of pedals—block pedals and rat trap pedals. Block pedals have rubber or plastic blocks that fit into a metal frame.

Rat trap pedals are all metal and have tiny teeth along the edges. They keep your feet from slipping off the pedal easily. Rat trap pedals are much safer than block pedals. Plus, you can fit rat trap pedals with a toe clip. With a toe clip, you get more power out of your pedaling.

The chainwheel on your bicycle is really a gear. Its teeth grab hold of your bicycle chain. So when you pedal, the chainwheel turns, making the chain move, too.

The Gears

Both the chainwheel and the freewheel on your bike are part of its gear system. The chainwheel is larger and has more teeth than the freewheel. So each time the chainwheel goes around once, the freewheel goes around a few times. You gain speed!

For example, a dirt bike might have 40 teeth on the chainwheel and 16 teeth on the freewheel. Each time you push the chainwheel around once with your pedals, the freewheel goes around 2 1/2 times. This is the simplest kind of gear.

Another kind of bike is a 3-speed. It has three different gears. Three-speed bikes have a shifting lever on the handlebars that you use to shift from one gear to another. When you press the shifter, a **derailleur** in the back wheel shifts the chain from one freewheel, or gearwheel, to another. Derailleurs help to shift the chain from gear to gear without getting jammed.

Each gearwheel is a different size. When you shift to a smaller gearwheel, you're in a higher gear. It's harder to pedal, but you get more speed. High gears are good when you really want to get moving.

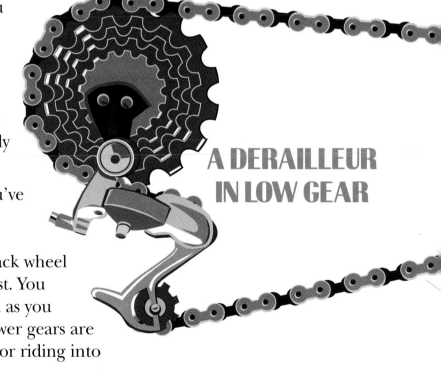

A DERAILLEUR IN LOW GEAR

Low gear means you've switched to a larger gearwheel. It's easier to pedal. However, your back wheel doesn't go around as fast. You can't get as much speed as you can in higher gears. Lower gears are great for going up hills or riding into the wind.

Bicycles with many speeds have more than one size of gearwheel *and* chainwheel. Today's most common bicycles are 10-speed, 18-speed, 21-speed and even 24-speed. A 10-speed bike, for example, has five gearwheels in the back, and two chainwheels. 2 X 5 = 10. How many gearwheels and chainwheels could a 21-speed bike have?

When you're in the highest gear, you use the largest chainwheel and the smallest gearwheel. It's really hard to pedal. When you're in the lowest gear you use the smallest chainwheel and the largest gearwheel. You can pedal so fast you're legs blur, but your bike hardly moves at all.

High-speed bicycles have two shift levers— one for the gearwheels and one for the chainwheels. Some even have electronic controls. You just press the numbered buttons to get the gear you want!

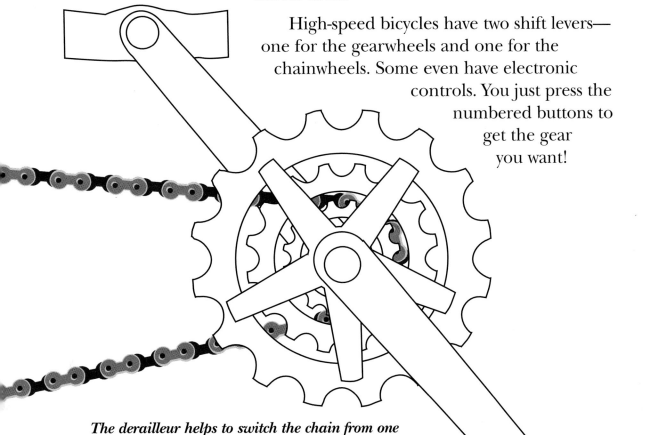

The derailleur helps to switch the chain from one gearwheel to another. In high gears, the chain goes around the largest chainwheel and the smallest gearwheel. In low gears, it goes around the smallest chainwheel and the largest gearwheel.

The Wheels

Even in high gear, if you don't have any wheels you won't go very far. The front wheel attaches to the fork and the back wheel attaches to the frame with nuts that tighten on a spindle. The wheels turn on the spindle and **bearings** inside the wheel **hub**(HUB).

Many bikes today come with wing nuts or a quick release lever. They let you take the wheels off easily, and without tools. Some bikes, like BMX and mountain bikes, come with **shock absorbers** (SHAHK ub SORB urz). The springs of simple shock absorbers help the rider get through rough territory. There are shock absorbers that use air and oil, or other materials, to do the same job.

Common sizes for bicycle wheels are 16-inch, 20-inch, 24-inch, 26-inch and 27-inch. Bicycle wheels are lightweight. However, they can carry a lot of weight. The spokes between the hub and the wheel rim help the bicycle hold up its load. Plus the spokes act as mini shock absorbers.

Riders choose tires depending on what they want to do with their bikes. Road racers like thin tires. Moto-cross racers and mountain bikers like thick tires with knobs or deep treads. However, all bikers need to make sure their tires are in good shape before they ride.

When you put on the brakes, the cable in a brake makes the brake shoes press against the wheel rims until your bike stops.

The Brakes

Speeding around on a bicycle is fun. However, how fast would you go if you knew you didn't have a way to stop? Brakes are a very important part of your bike. You should always check them before you ride.

There are several kinds of brakes for bicycles. Your first bike probably had a **coaster brake** (KOHS tur BRAYK). You push your pedal backward to stop. Back pedaling makes the chain ride back on the chainwheel. Then the chain forces the rear **axle** against the brake arm. The brake arm pushes against your back wheel until it stops, or until you stop braking.

Today, most bikes use **caliper brakes** (KA luh pur BRAYKS). Caliper rim brakes have a brake on the back and front tires. Thin cables run between the brake levers on your handlebars and the brakes on the wheel rims.

When you pull on the brake levers, the brake cables make the brake shoes press against the wheel rims. The harder you squeeze, the harder the brake shoes squeeze the rims until you stop. When you let go of the brake levers, a spring in the brake pulls the brake shoes away from the wheels.

19

A Balancing Act

Do you remember what it was like when you were learning how to ride your bike? You probably swerved and wobbled—and you might have had a spill or two.

What was the problem? Why is it so easy now to hop on your bike and go? Your body has learned the secret of balance. Plus the science of physics and motion is helping you, too.

When you were just starting to ride, you were probably a little scared. So, you went very slow. The truth is going slow makes it harder for you to balance! You can see how this works by playing around with a gyroscope.

Once you get a gyroscope going, it stays upright for a long time—as long as its wheel keeps spinning. In fact, if you hold a spinning gyroscope in your hand and try to tip it, it fights you. It doesn't want to change direction. It will wobble or even jump out of your hand. The gyroscope wants to stay upright.

A bicycle acts like a giant gyroscope. As you ride, your wheels are spinning, gaining momentum. The faster you go, the faster your wheels spin and the more momentum you have.

The spinning wheels also have inertia. That means that they want to keep spinning. The moving bike has inertia, too. It wants to keep going. Momentum and inertia make bicycle wheels resist any change in direction.

When you're pedaling your bicycle, your spinning wheels want to stay upright, just like the gyroscope in your hand. So, the faster you go, the harder it is to fall—unless you run into something! Thanks to the rules of physics—momentum and inertia—a moving bicycle actually helps you balance.

CHAPTER FOUR

KINDS OF BICYCLES

Bicycles today are not really a whole lot different than they were 100 years ago. The frames, wheels, pedals, **gears,** seats and handlebars all work pretty much the same.

Moto-cross racers use sturdy BMX bikes with small frames and thick tires. Shock absorbers on the front wheel help make the ride a little easier.

What makes modern bicycles so exciting is the way they're made, and the many ways they are used. Lighter materials make bicycles much lighter and more streamlined than ever. More gear options give riders more choices in how and where they ride.

Here are a few of the bikes you might see on the road—or off the road—today.

Street Bikes

For many years, this was the kind of bike every kid had. Street bikes have heavy frames and 26-inch wheels with balloon tires. They can be 1-speed or 3-speed with **coaster brakes** or **caliper brakes.** The handlebars curve back toward the rider.

Street bikes were made for just that—riding around the streets. The heavy frames lasted for a long time.

BMX Bikes

If you like dirt track racing, the BMX bike is the bike for you. BMX bikes have short, sturdy frames on 20-inch wheels. The tires are wide and knobby for gripping the dirt. The handlebars are straight with caliper breaks.

BMX bikes are single-speed bikes. That means they have a single **chainwheel** and a single **freewheel.** Good BMX bikes have a **shock absorber** system for the front wheel. BMX bikes have to cover a lot of rough ground.

Mountain Bikes

A mountain bike is another kind of off-road bike. It is built for racing and riding in the mountains. It has a sturdy, lightweight frame on 26-inch wheels. Like a BMX bike, its tires are wide and have a deep **tread** (TRED). It also has strong shock absorbers.

However, mountain bikes have many gears. Shifting gears helps mountain bike riders deal with different slopes as they go up and down mountains. The handlebars are straight with easy-to-reach shifting levers and brake levers.

Instead of caliper brakes, some mountain bikes have a **cantilever brake** (KAN tu lee vur BRAYK) system. Cantilever brake systems are sturdier than caliper brakes, and work better for mountain bikes. Each brake shoe works on its own, instead of in pairs, as with a caliper brake. Cantilever brakes really hold up to the bouncing and jolting of rough mountain bike riding.

The First Bicycle Race

Kirkpatric Macmillan was the first person to build a modern bicycle. He was a Scottish engineer, and he called his invention a velocipede. On May 30, 1869, people raced velocipedes through the Parc de Saint-Cloud in Paris, France. The race was 1,200 meters long.

Racing And Touring Bikes

When someone says *racing bike* almost everyone gets the same picture. They are the sleek, very lightweight bikes that zip down the roads of famous races like the Tour de France. The frame is much narrower than other bikes. Their 27-inch wheels are also very narrow.

The dropped handles on a racing bike let the rider crouch low. Riding low means less wind resistance and higher speeds. Racing bikes are 10-speed or higher. Most serious racers build their own bikes, or have them built by specialists.

Touring, or road, bikes are like racing bikes, but not so expensive. Speed is not as important in touring bikes, so the frames are not quite as light.

People who take long bike trips usually use a touring bike. They can add things to their bikes to make their trips safer and easier. Tall poles with flags make touring bikes easy to see in traffic. You can buy carriers like baskets or bags, water bottles, tool kits and rear view mirrors to add on, too.

The thin tires and light frames give road racers a way to increase their speeds.

Cross Or Hybrid Bikes

Cross bikes, also called hybrids, are like a mountain bike and a touring bike combined. Cross bikes look like mountain bikes. However, the frame is usually a little heavier.

Mostly people in towns and cities choose to buy cross bikes. They often buy the same kinds of things that people put on touring bikes. You might also see lights and fenders on cross bikes. Cross bikes work great for people who may like to go off-road on a bike path, but will probably never bike in the mountains.

INVENTORS ON THE MOVE

Bicycles are a simple machine. Over the years inventors have taken this simple machine and changed it into all sorts of fantastic creations.

Fun Bikes

All bikes are fun. However, there is a special kind of bike called a fun bike. People use fun bikes for trick riding.

These bikes have a heavy frame, banana seat and high handlebars. They are very low, with 20-inch wheels. To give a trick rider lots of control, they have caliper brakes, wide deep-tread tires and several gears.

Tandem Bikes

Tandem (TAN dum) bikes are bicycles built for two. They have been around for more than 100 years. There are two sets of handlebars, two sets of pedals and two seats. Only the person in front can steer. The back handlebars are there for the other person to hang onto. They can come with a single speed or many speeds.

Tandem bikes can do one very special job. With a tandem bike, a blind, or visually impaired, person can enjoy bike riding with a sighted partner.

Blast From A Bike's Past

On June 7, 1897, 11 cadets from Northwestern Military Academy, Lake Geneva, Wisconsin, left Chicago, Illinois, on bicycles. They began a mission to deliver a message to Washington, D.C. Twenty-one days later, Russell Alexander, Secretary of Defense, received his message.

CHAPTER FIVE

SAFETY AND CARE OF BICYCLES

A bicycle is a simple machine that's a lot of fun to use. It can take you farther and faster than walking and give you some good exercise. However, your bicycle needs you even more than you need it.

Taking Care Of Business

When you buy a bicycle, it usually comes with an owner's manual. Read it. This manual will tell you how to keep your bike in good working order. It will tell you how to put all the pieces together, and how often you need a tune-up.

If you didn't get, or can't find, the manual for your bike, try checking out a book from the library. Books like these will have simple drawings and give you helpful tips on taking care of your bike's business.

Tire pumps are better for bike tires than air compressors. Air compressors can fill a tire too full, and could damage your tire.

For example, before you take a ride, you should do a mini inspection. Check your tires to see that they have enough air. If you need to, use a tire pump to pump up your tire to the right pressure. You'll find the right pressure printed on the side of the tire. Also check the tires and rims for any signs of leaks or wearing.

Before you go too far, you should also test your brakes.

About once a month, you should check all the nuts, screws and bolts to make sure they're tight. The handlebars should be tight, and so should the handle grips. Inspect your bike's frame. The front fork should be straight.

Do a thorough brake check. The brake shoes should not be worn. They should not be too far from, or too close to, the wheel rim. Check to make sure the brake cables are in good shape, too.

Then turn your bike over and spin the wheels. Make sure they don't wobble. Look for loose or broken spokes in both wheels. Check your pedals. They should spin freely.

Finally test your seat. Is it still at the right height for you? It should fit tightly in place, and be pointed in the right direction.

Knowing about your bike makes you a better bike rider. If you need help getting to know your bike, try visiting a bicycle shop. Repair shops can service your bike and make sure it's still safe to ride.

More Than Pedal Power

Special bicycles, called mopeds, have both pedals and a small engine. Some run on gasoline, and others run on electricity. Mopeds have a cruising speed of about 30 mph.

Riding Responsibility

Bicycles are wonderful machines, if you know how to use them. Once you've found the right bike for you, first practice riding off busy roads. Give yourself time to get your balance and learn the rules of the road.

Riding a bike means you follow some of the same rules as car drivers. Unless there is a bike path, you should ride on the right side of the road. You need to signal when you are going to stop, turn right or turn left. If you are riding with a group of friends, ride single file.

Sometimes people in cars and trucks have a hard time seeing bicycles. You can help by adding a headlight and reflectors to your bike. At night it's a good idea to put reflector tape on your clothing. However, you should always wear a helmet—day or night.

Bicycling with friends can be a lot of fun, but don't forget that you're on the road. You should keep your eyes out for cars and trucks. You can see them easier than they can see you. Stay alert! You have much more control if you keep both hands on the handlebars, and don't ride double.

There are many safe places to ride your bike. Off major highways, many country roads have little traffic and lots of great scenery. More and more cities and states are building bike lanes. Today there are over 300,000 miles of trails and 'marked routes in the U.S. just for bicycles.

Using signals like these helps the people in cars know what you plan to do.

Whether you're going for a long ride or a short one, you should always wear your helmet.

Electrified Bikes

Motorized bikes are not a new idea. However, a new kind of motorized bike, developed by a company called Sanyo, uses an electric motor. Like electric cars, this bike's motor is more energy efficient and environment-friendly than earlier mopeds.

The *Warrior* looks like a mountain bike with a plastic box behind the seat and over the back tire. Using just the motor, riders can go about 15 mph. If they pedal, they can go up to 20 mph.

This electrified bike is powered by two 24-volt electric motors and two rechargeable 12-volt batteries. It takes about 30 minutes to charge them, and weighs about 30 pounds.

alloy (A loy) - a mixture of two or more metals; made by melting them together

axle (AK sul) - rod, or shaft, on which a wheel turns

bearings (BAYR ingz) - metal balls that reduce friction, or make something easier to turn; usually held in a ring or ring-shaped cup

caliper brakes (KA luh pur BRAYKS) - type of wheel rim brake on a bicycle; made up of two curved arms that are bolted together on the frame; they operate using a lever and cable system

cantilever brakes (KAN tu lee vur BRAYKS) - type of wheel rim brake on a bicycle, made up of single curved arms and bolted to the frame at the end of each arm; they operate using a lever and cable system

chainwheel (CHAYN weel) - chain ring; large pedal sprocket on a bicycle

coaster brake (KOHS tur BRAYK) - type of bicycle brake; it works when you back pedal

crank (KRANK) - a bent arm or shaft for turning a wheel; the pedal arm of a bicycle that turns the chainwheel

derailleur (di RAY lur) - gear shifting device on a bicycle; it shifts the bicycle chain between different size gearwheels and chainwheels

freewheel (FREE weel) - on a bicycle, a rear wheel sprocket that allows the rear wheel to turn without pedaling, while the bike coasts

gear (GEER) - toothed wheel used to change force or direction; the sprocket on a bicycle

generator (JEH nuh ray tur) - a motor that changes motion into electricity

hub (HUB) - the center part of a wheel; all the spokes of a bicycle wheel come together at the hub

microprocessor (mii kroh PRAHS es ur) - a mini computer

security (si KYUR uh tee) - safety; things you do to protect against harm or theft

shock absorbers (SHAHK ub SORB urz) - a device that makes the bumps and jolts of riding seem smaller

sprocket (SPRAH kut) - wheel with teeth around the rim, used with a chain

tandem (TAN dum) - a bicycle built for two

tread (TRED) - the part of a tire that touches the road

INDEX